Date: 11/15/22

**PALM BEACH COUNTY
LIBRARY SYSTEM**

**3650 Summit Boulevard
West Palm Beach, FL 33406**

Y0-CUO-319

Dr. Seuss

by Julie Murray

Abdo
CHILDREN'S AUTHORS
Kids

Abdo Kids Jumbo is an Imprint of Abdo Kids
abdobooks.com

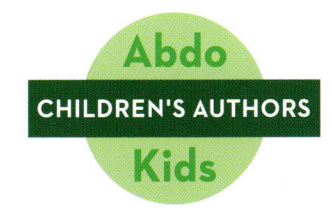

abdobooks.com

Published by Abdo Kids, a division of ABDO, P.O. Box 398166, Minneapolis, Minnesota 55439. Copyright © 2022 by Abdo Consulting Group, Inc. International copyrights reserved in all countries. No part of this book may be reproduced in any form without written permission from the publisher. Abdo Kids Jumbo™ is a trademark and logo of Abdo Kids.

Printed in the United States of America, North Mankato, Minnesota.

102021

012022

THIS BOOK CONTAINS RECYCLED MATERIALS

Photo Credits: Alamy, AP Images, Everette Collection, Getty Images, iStock, newscom, Seth Poppel/Yearbook Library, Shutterstock

Production Contributors: Teddy Borth, Jennie Forsberg, Grace Hansen
Design Contributors: Candice Keimig, Pakou Moua

Library of Congress Control Number: 2020948018

Publisher's Cataloging-in-Publication Data

Names: Murray, Julie, author.

Title: Dr. Seuss / by Julie Murray

Description: Minneapolis, Minnesota : Abdo Kids, 2022 | Series: Children's authors | Includes online resources and index.

Identifiers: ISBN 9781098207212 (lib. bdg.) | ISBN 9781098208059 (ebook) | ISBN 9781098208479 (Read-to-Me ebook)

Subjects: LCSH: Seuss, Dr.--Juvenile literature. | Geisel, Theodor Seuss, 1904-1991--Juvenile literature. | Authors--Biography--Juvenile literature. | Children's books--Juvenile literature.

Classification: DDC 809.8928--dc23

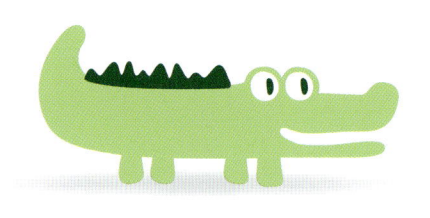

Table of Contents

Early Years 4

Stories 10

Death & Legacy 18

Timeline. 22

Glossary 23

Index 24

Abdo Kids Code. 24

Early Years

Theodor Seuss Geisel was born on March 2, 1904, in Springfield, Massachusetts. People called him Ted.

Springfield, Massachusetts

Ted's father worked at a zoo. Ted often visited. He loved to draw pictures of the animals. He drew them using funny shapes.

7

Ted wrote for a school magazine in college. He signed his work with his middle name "Seuss." He later added the "Dr." and "Dr. Seuss" became his pen name.

9

Stories

Ted loved creating books with rhymes and funny characters. He published his first book in 1937. Less than a year later, he released his next book, *The 500 Hats of Bartholomew Cubbins*.

11

Horton Hears a Who was published in 1954. It is about an elephant named Horton that tries to save the tiny town of **Whoville**. Horton starred on the big screen in 2008.

13

In 1957, *How the Grinch Stole Christmas* was published. Ted saw himself in the Grinch and wanted to change. He wanted people to celebrate Christmas with love instead of just gifts.

15

Ted also created books that were easy to read. He wrote *The Cat in the Hat*. He also wrote *Green Eggs and Ham* using just 50 words.

17

Death & Legacy

Theodor Seuss Geisel died on September 24, 1991. He had written and **illustrated** more than 40 books. He won many awards, including a **Pulitzer Prize** in 1984.

19

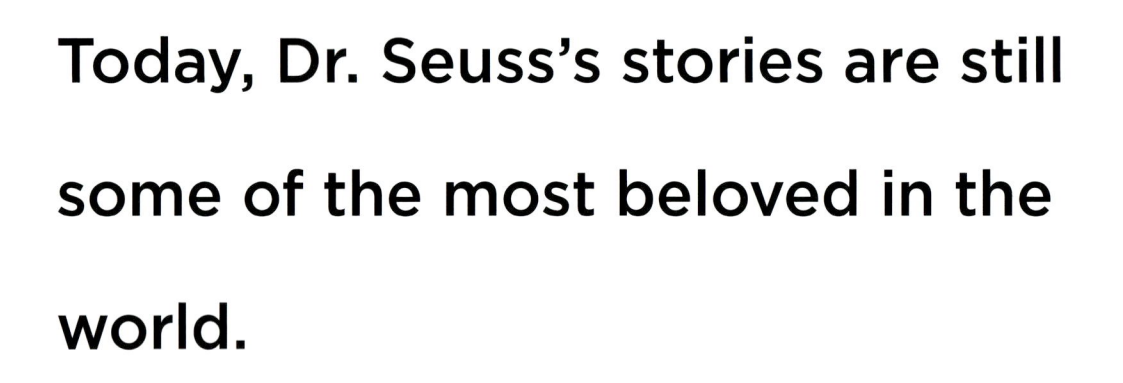

Today, Dr. Seuss's stories are still some of the most beloved in the world.

21

Timeline

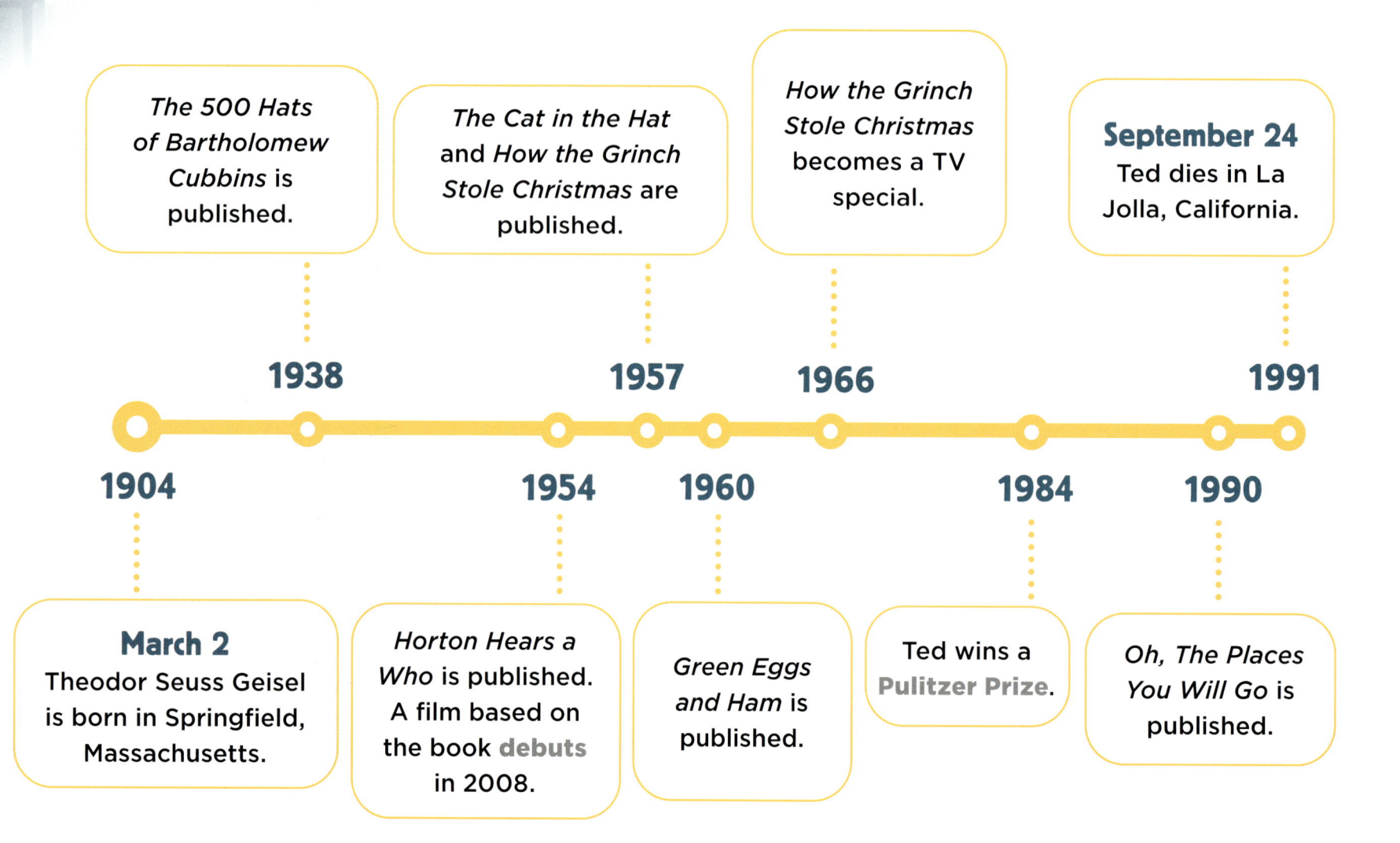

1904 — **March 2** Theodor Seuss Geisel is born in Springfield, Massachusetts.

1938 — *The 500 Hats of Bartholomew Cubbins* is published.

1954 — *Horton Hears a Who* is published. A film based on the book **debuts** in 2008.

1957 — *The Cat in the Hat* and *How the Grinch Stole Christmas* are published.

1960 — *Green Eggs and Ham* is published.

1966 — *How the Grinch Stole Christmas* becomes a TV special.

1984 — Ted wins a **Pulitzer Prize**.

1990 — *Oh, The Places You Will Go* is published.

1991 — **September 24** Ted dies in La Jolla, California.

22

Glossary

debut – to present to an audience for the first time.

illustrate – to draw pictures to go along with a book or other written material.

pen name – a name used by authors in place of their real names.

Pulitzer Prize – any of several prizes established by journalist Joseph Pulitzer and awarded for outstanding achievement to U.S. journalists, authors, playwrights, and composers.

Whoville – a fictional town created by Dr. Seuss that is filled with citizens called Whos.

Index

500 Hats of Batholomew Cubbins, The 10

awards 18

birth 4

Cat in the Hat, The 16

death 20

education 8

family 6

film 12

Green Eggs and Ham 16

Horton Hears a Who 12

How the Grinch Stole Christmas 14

Massachusetts 4

works 10, 12, 14, 16, 20

Abdo Kids ONLINE
FREE! ONLINE MULTIMEDIA RESOURCES

Visit **abdokids.com** to access crafts, games, videos, and more!

Use Abdo Kids code **CDK7212** or scan this QR code!